BUFFALO BILLS

MATT SCHEFF

Apex is distributed by North Star Editions:
sales@northstareditions.com | 888-417-0195

Produced for Apex by Red Line Editorial.

Photographs ©: Paul Spinelli/AP Images, cover, 1; Kevin Sabitus/Getty Images Sport/Getty Images, 4–5; Adrian Kraus/AP Images, 6–7; Hy Peskin Archive/Archive Photos/Getty Images, 8–9; Charles Aqua Viva/Getty Images Sport/Getty Images, 10–11; J. Spencer Jones/AP Images, 12–13; Mark Duncan/AP Images, 14–15; Paul Spinelli/NFL Photos/AP Images, 16–17, 58–59; David Durochik/AP Images, 19, 57; Herb Scharfman/Sports Imagery/Getty Images Sport/Getty Images, 20–21; Tony Tomsic/AP Images, 22–23; Rick Stewart/Allsport/Getty Images Sport/Getty Images, 24–25, 29, 30–31; Al Bello/Getty Images Sport/Getty Images, 26–27; Tom Szczerbowski/Getty Images Sport/Getty Images, 32–33, 38–39; Jamie Squire/Getty Images Sport/Getty Images, 34–35; Joshua Bessex/AP Images, 36–37; Tim Warner/Getty Images Sport/Getty Images, 40–41; Bryan Bennett/Getty Images Sport/Getty Images, 42–43; Timothy T. Ludwig/Getty Images Sport/Getty Images, 44–45; Shutterstock Images, 47, 48–49; Joshua Bessex/Getty Images Sport/Getty Images, 50–51; Doug Murray/AP Images, 52–53; Joe Robbins/AP Images, 54–55

Library of Congress Control Number: 2023921774

ISBN
979-8-89250-078-4 (hardcover)
979-8-89250-095-1 (paperback)
979-8-89250-128-6 (ebook pdf)
979-8-89250-112-5 (hosted ebook)

Printed in the United States of America
Mankato, MN
082024

NOTE TO PARENTS AND EDUCATORS

Apex books are designed to build literacy skills in striving readers. Exciting, high-interest content attracts and holds readers' attention. The text is carefully leveled to allow students to achieve success quickly.

TABLE OF CONTENTS

CHAPTER 1

RIGHT HERE, RIGHT NOW

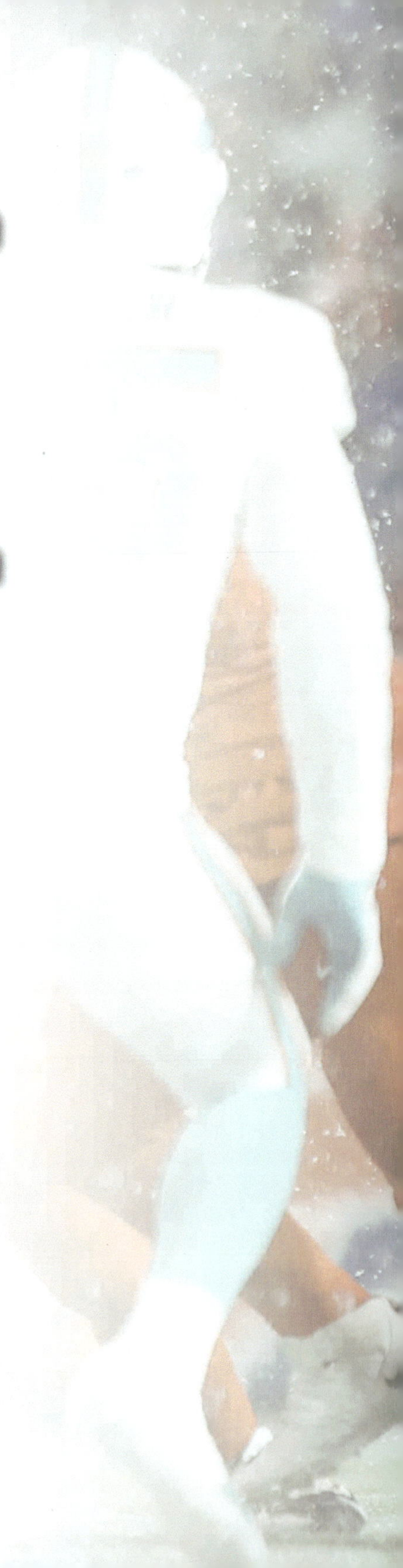

Snow falls on the Buffalo Bills' stadium. Thousands of fans rise to their feet. They stomp and cheer. Their team marches down the field. The Bills are trailing. They need a touchdown.

Bills quarterback Josh Allen looks for a receiver during a 2022 game against the Miami Dolphins.

Buffalo wide receiver Dawson Knox catches a touchdown pass from Josh Allen.

Quarterback Josh Allen takes the snap. He drops back and scans the field. Suddenly, he spots an open receiver in the end zone.

Allen lofts a pass. The receiver hauls it in. It's a touchdown! The fans go wild.

FIRED UP

In the 1980s, head coach Marv Levy gave a speech to his players. He said, "Where else would you rather be than right here, right now?" Bills fans started using the phrase. Today, the whole stadium shouts it before games.

CHAPTER 2

EARLY HISTORY

The AFL formed in 1960. This league was separate from the NFL. The AFL started with eight teams. One of them was the Buffalo Bills. At first, things weren't easy for the Bills. They struggled during their first three seasons.

In their first two seasons, the Bills wore silver and blue uniforms.

Buffalo running back Billy Joe (33) takes a handoff during the 1965 AFL title game.

The team turned a corner in 1963. Buffalo tied for first place in its division. And the Bills kept getting better. They soon became the league's top team. The Bills won the AFL title in 1964. They won another title in 1965.

ALL-AMERICANS

The Bills weren't the first football team in Buffalo. The city had a team in the early 1900s. The Buffalo All-Americans joined the NFL when it formed in 1920. A few years later, they changed their name to the Bisons. The team shut down in 1929.

The AFL and NFL competed for players. They also competed for fans. So, in 1966, the two leagues agreed to merge. In 1970, the AFL became part of the NFL. But the change wasn't easy for the Bills. The team won just four games in its first two NFL seasons.

WHAT'S IN A NAME?

The Bills take their name from "Buffalo" Bill Cody. He lived from the mid-1800s to the early 1900s. Cody was a bison hunter in the American West. He later became a famous showman.

The Bills struggled against the New York Giants during a game in 1970.

The Bills had a strong running game in the 1970s. But it didn't result in many wins. Buffalo made the playoffs only once that decade.

In 1986, the Bills hired head coach Marv Levy. He helped bring success to Buffalo. The Bills made the playoffs in 1988 and 1989. And after the 1990 season, they reached their first Super Bowl. They faced the New York Giants. The Bills had a chance to win. But they missed a field goal on their final play.

In the 1990 season, Buffalo crushed the Los Angeles Raiders 51–3 in the playoffs.

The Bills won many games in the early 1990s. Their offense used a fast-paced, no-huddle style. It kept other teams off-balance. The Bills went to four straight Super Bowls. However, they lost all four.

Buffalo took on the Dallas Cowboys in two straight Super Bowls.

EPIC COMEBACK

In the 1992 season, Buffalo faced the Houston Oilers in the playoffs. Buffalo trailed 35–3 in the third quarter. But backup quarterback Frank Reich led the Bills all the way back. Buffalo won the game 41–38 in overtime.

PLAYER SPOTLIGHT

BRUCE SMITH

Bruce Smith was the first pick of the 1985 NFL Draft. He soon became the heart of the Bills defense. His speed and strength made him almost impossible to block.

Smith's best season came in 1990. He had a career-high 19 sacks. He also earned the Defensive Player of the Year Award.

Smith spent 15 seasons with the Bills. During that time, he recorded 171 sacks. Smith entered the Pro Football Hall of Fame in 2009.

BRUCE SMITH MADE THE PRO BOWL IN 11 OF HIS 15 SEASONS WITH BUFFALO.

CHAPTER 3

LEGENDS

Quarterback Jack Kemp was one of the first Bills legends. He led the team to AFL titles in 1964 and 1965. Kemp played behind a strong offensive line. Guard Billy Shaw was one of the best blockers in the league.

In 1965, Jack Kemp (15) earned the AFL's Most Valuable Player Award.

In the 1970s, Buffalo's biggest star was running back O. J. Simpson. In 1973, Simpson ran for 2,003 yards. He did it in just 14 games. Simpson was the first player to reach the 2,000-yard mark. But he didn't do it alone. Guard Joe DeLamielleure led a powerful offensive line. "Joe D" was durable. In eight seasons with Buffalo, he never missed a game.

In the 1970s, the Bills' offensive line was nicknamed the "Electric Company."

In the 1990s, quarterback Jim Kelly led Buffalo's no-huddle offense. He had plenty of help. Running back Thurman Thomas was great at both running and catching. Wide receiver Andre Reed was a scoring machine. He recorded 87 touchdowns with the Bills.

MOST VALUABLE PLAYER

Thurman Thomas had his best season in 1991. He racked up 1,407 yards on the ground. He also had 631 receiving yards. That put his total at 2,038 yards. Thomas won the Most Valuable Player (MVP) Award.

Thurman Thomas scored 65 rushing touchdowns and 22 receiving touchdowns for the Bills.

The Bills of the 1990s were known for offense. But their defense was strong, too. Bruce Smith was one of the greatest pass rushers of all time. Linebackers Cornelius Bennett and Darryl Talley were also excellent tacklers.

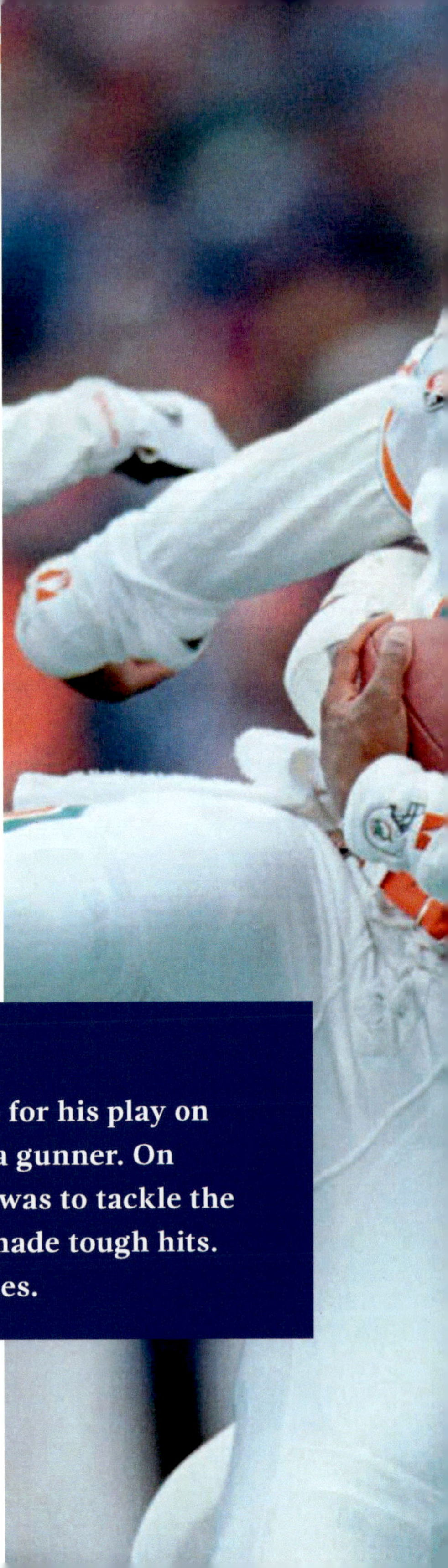

TOP GUNNER

Steve Tasker is best known for his play on special teams. Tasker was a gunner. On kickoffs and punts, his job was to tackle the return man. Tasker often made tough hits. He also forced many fumbles.

Cornelius Bennett earned five trips to the Pro Bowl as a member of the Bills.

PLAYER SPOTLIGHT

JIM KELLY

Quarterback Jim Kelly joined the Bills in 1986. Before long, he became a star. He led Buffalo's no-huddle offense in the 1990s. Kelly was great at making quick decisions. He also spread the ball around to different receivers. That made Buffalo's offense hard to defend.

Kelly's best season came in 1991. He led the NFL with 33 touchdown passes. He also finished second in MVP voting. Kelly spent 11 years with the Bills. In 2002, he entered the Pro Football Hall of Fame.

JIM KELLY THREW 237 TOUCHDOWN PASSES DURING HIS CAREER.

CHAPTER 4

RECENT HISTORY

Jim Kelly retired after the 1996 season. Buffalo's era of greatness soon ended. From 2000 to 2016, the team didn't make the playoffs once. Even so, Bills fans kept cheering for their team.

Quarterback Doug Flutie led Buffalo to the playoffs in the 1999 season.

In 2017, the Bills hired head coach Sean McDermott. He quickly turned the team around. In his first season, McDermott led the Bills to the playoffs. The next year, Buffalo drafted quarterback Josh Allen. The stage was set for a return to the top.

ENDING THE DROUGHT

The Bills struggled in the 2000s and early 2010s. By 2016, they had gone 17 years without making the playoffs. At the time, it was the longest playoff drought in North American sports. Sean McDermott helped end that streak.

Before he joined the Bills, Sean McDermott spent many years as a defensive coach for the Carolina Panthers.

In 2020, the Bills went 13–3. However, they lost to the Kansas City Chiefs in the playoffs. A year later, the two teams met again. Buffalo took the lead with just 13 seconds left. But the Chiefs stormed back and tied the game. Kansas City won in overtime. It was a crushing loss for Bills fans.

Gabriel Davis (13) scored four touchdowns in Buffalo's loss to Kansas City in January 2022.

The Bills were great again in 2022. They went 13–3 in the regular season. But once again, the season ended in heartbreak. Buffalo lost to the Cincinnati Bengals in the playoffs. The 2023 season ended with another tough loss. The Bills fell to the Chiefs in the playoffs.

SAVING DAMAR

In the 2022 season, Buffalo safety Damar Hamlin collapsed during a game. His heart had stopped. Doctors rushed onto the field. They saved his life. Hamlin recovered in the hospital. The football world cheered him on. In 2023, Hamlin returned as a member of the Bills.

Bills players and fans show their support for Damar Hamlin.

CHAPTER 5

MODERN STARS

Defensive tackle Kyle Williams was the heart of the Bills defense in the 2010s. From 2010 to 2018, Williams made six Pro Bowls. His size and strength made him a great run-stopper. He could also bring down the quarterback. In 2013, he racked up 10.5 sacks.

Kyle Williams (95) spent his entire 13-year career with the Bills.

Running back LeSean McCoy spent just four years with the Bills. But he made them count. McCoy was one of the league's best runners. He was very fast. And he could avoid tackles. That made him a nightmare for defenses.

ERIC MOULDS

Eric Moulds was a big receiver. He had great hands, too. Defenses had a hard time stopping him. Moulds spent 10 years with the Bills. He scored 49 touchdowns during that time.

LeSean McCoy (25) bursts through the line during a 2018 game against the Houston Texans.

Stefon Diggs was a star before he joined the Bills. He became a top receiver with the Minnesota Vikings. The Bills traded for him in 2020. Along with Josh Allen, Diggs helped turn Buffalo into a winner. Diggs could get open on long routes and short routes. That made him a huge threat. In 2020, Diggs led the NFL in both catches and receiving yards.

Stefon Diggs (14) makes an amazing catch against the New England Patriots.

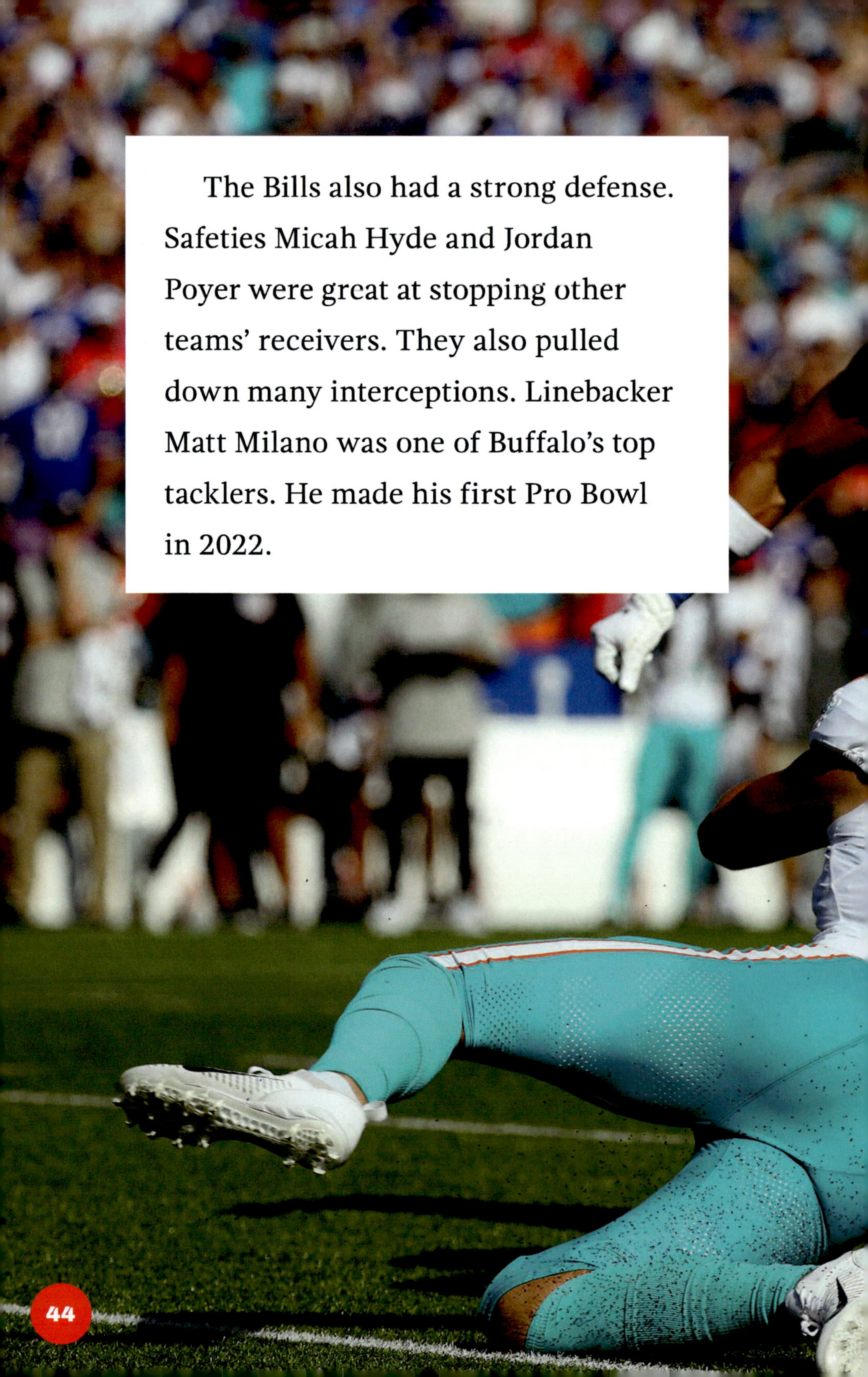

The Bills also had a strong defense. Safeties Micah Hyde and Jordan Poyer were great at stopping other teams' receivers. They also pulled down many interceptions. Linebacker Matt Milano was one of Buffalo's top tacklers. He made his first Pro Bowl in 2022.

Micah Hyde (23) runs back an interception during a 2023 game against Miami.

PLAYER SPOTLIGHT

JOSH ALLEN

Josh Allen was a star at the University of Wyoming. The Bills chose him in the 2018 NFL Draft. Allen soon became one of the best dual-threat quarterbacks in the NFL. He could win games with his strong arm. He could also use his size and speed to run the ball. It was a tough combination for defenses to stop.

Allen became a star in his third NFL season. He threw 37 touchdown passes that year. He also finished second in MVP voting.

JOSH ALLEN LED 11 FOURTH-QUARTER COMEBACKS IN HIS FIRST FIVE SEASONS WITH BUFFALO.

BILLS
17
NFL

CHAPTER 6

TEAM TRIVIA

Three NFL teams call New York State their home. But the New York Giants play their home games in New Jersey. So do the New York Jets. That means the Bills are the only NFL team that actually plays in New York.

For many years, Buffalo's stadium was named after Ralph Wilson, the team's first owner.

A fan known as "Pinto Ron" gets covered in condiments before every game.

Buffalo fans are known as the Bills Mafia. Many fans like to tailgate before games. Sometimes things get wild in the parking lot. One fan lets people cover him in ketchup and mustard!

BILLY BUFFALO

The Bills' mascot is Billy Buffalo. He first appeared in 2000. The bright-blue buffalo helps fans get fired up during games. Billy also takes part in other events. Some fans even invite him to their weddings.

LIFE AFTER FOOTBALL

Quarterback Jack Kemp had a great career with the Bills. After he stopped playing, he became a lawmaker. Kemp served in the US Congress for 18 years.

At home games, the song "Shout" plays every time Buffalo scores. If the Bills win, "Shout" plays after the game, too. The team also has a song called "Go Bills." Head coach Marv Levy wrote it in the 1990s.

The Bills have been playing "Shout" since 1987.

Some fans wear costumes and face paint to games.

Bills fans are also well known for their sportsmanship. In 2017, Bengals quarterback Andy Dalton threw a touchdown. That helped the Bengals beat the Baltimore Ravens. As a result, Buffalo made the playoffs. Bills fans gave thousands of dollars to Dalton's charity.

In 2018, a Chicago TV station made fun of Bills fans. But people in Buffalo didn't get angry. Instead, they donated money to a charity in Chicago.

TEAM RECORDS

All-Time Passing Yards: 35,467
Jim Kelly (1986–96)

All-Time Touchdown Passes: 237
Jim Kelly (1986–96)

All-Time Rushing Yards: 11,938
Thurman Thomas (1988–99)

All-Time Receiving Yards: 13,095
Andre Reed (1985–99)

All-Time Interceptions: 40
Butch Byrd (1964–70)

All-Time Sacks: 171
Bruce Smith (1985–99)

All-Time Scoring: 1,011
Steve Christie (1992–2000)

All-Time Games Played: 221
Andre Reed (1985–99)

All-Time Coaching Wins: 112
Marv Levy (1986–97)

AFL Titles: 2
(1964, 1965)

All statistics are accurate through 2023.

TIMELINE

1960

The Bills join the newly formed AFL.

1964

The Bills win their first AFL championship.

1965

Buffalo beats the San Diego Chargers 23–0 to win a second straight AFL title.

1970

The AFL and NFL merge. The Bills become part of the NFL's American Football Conference (AFC).

1973

O. J. Simpson becomes the first running back to rush for 2,000 yards in a season.

1990

The Bills make the first of four straight Super Bowl appearances.

2017

The Bills hire Sean McDermott as head coach. He helps end a 17-year playoff drought.

2018

Buffalo selects quarterback Josh Allen in the first round of the NFL Draft.

2020

The Bills lose to the Kansas City Chiefs in the conference championship game.

2022

Safety Damar Hamlin collapses on the field. Medical staff rush out and save his life.

COMPREHENSION QUESTIONS

Write your answers on a separate piece of paper.

1. Write a paragraph that explains the main ideas in Chapter 4.

2. Who do you think is the best player in Bills history? Why?

3. Which quarterback led the Bills to two AFL titles?

   A. Jim Kelly
   B. Josh Allen
   C. Jack Kemp

4. Why are Bills fans known for their sportsmanship?

   A. They have wild parties before games.
   B. They raise money for other teams' charities.
   C. They have a bright-blue mascot.

5. What does **durable** mean in this book?

*"Joe D" was **durable**. In eight seasons with Buffalo, he never missed a game.*

A. strong and healthy
B. easy to tackle
C. very exciting

6. What does **dual-threat** mean in this book?

*Allen soon became one of the best **dual-threat** quarterbacks in the NFL. He could win games with his strong arm. He could also use his size and speed to run the ball.*

A. a quarterback who is good at running and throwing
B. a quarterback who can throw with either arm
C. a quarterback who also plays defense

Answer key on page 64.

GLOSSARY

draft
A system that lets teams select new players coming into the league.

league
A group of teams that play one another and compete for a championship.

merge
To join two leagues together.

no-huddle
When players do not gather together to plan the next play.

retired
Ended one's career.

routes
Paths that receivers take so they can get open and catch the ball.

sacks
Plays that happen when a defender tackles the quarterback before he can throw the ball.

special teams
The players who are on the field during kicks and punts.

sportsmanship
Competing in a fair and respectful way.

tailgate
To gather in a parking lot before a game, usually with food.

TO LEARN MORE

BOOKS

Abdo, Kenny. *Buffalo Bills*. Minneapolis: Abdo Publishing, 2022.

Downs, Kieran. *The Buffalo Bills*. Minneapolis: Bellwether Media, 2024.

Lowe, Alexander. *Josh Allen*. Minneapolis: Lerner Publications, 2022.

ONLINE RESOURCES

Visit **www.apexeditions.com** to find links and resources related to this title.

ABOUT THE AUTHOR

Matt Scheff is an author and artist living in Alaska. He enjoys mountain climbing, fishing, and curling up with his two Siberian huskies to watch sports.

INDEX

ANSWER KEY:

1. Answers will vary; 2. Answers will vary; 3. C; 4. B; 5. A; 6. A